Take a trip to CHINA

Text and photographs by

Sally Mason

General Editor

Henry Pluckrose

Franklin Watts
London   New York   Sydney   Toronto

Words about China

Beijing
Beijing Duck
bronze coins
Buddhism

Chinese
chopsticks
communes
communist

Emperor

fen
Forbidden City

Great Wall of
China

Hangzhou
hutung

Imperial Palace

jiao
junks

Liu Ho Pagoda

Mongol

paddy fields
pagodas
Peking
People's Daily

Red Silk Dance
rice

Shanghai
silk embroidery
steamed bread
symbol

taiji
temples
Tiananmen
Square
Tibetan

yuan
Young Pioneers

Some towns and cities in China have new spellings. The
map gives both spellings, the new with the old spelling
underneath. In the text, both spellings are given initially
(the old one in brackets) after which only the new
spelling appears.

Franklin Watts Limited
8 Cork Street
London W1

ISBN UK edition: 0 851 928X
ISBN US edition: 0 531 04317 7
Library of Congress Catalog Card No:
81–50029

© Franklin Watts Limited 1981

Printed in Great Britain by
E. T. Heron, Essex and London

The author and publisher would like to
thank the following for kind permission to
reproduce photographs: Allan Friedmann
(front cover, pages 9, 29); Julian
Friedmann (pages 25, 26); Xinhua News
Agency (pages 8, 12, 15, 28).

Maps by Brian and Constance Dear, and
Tony Payne

Design by Heather Sherratt

More people live in the People's Republic of China than in any other country in the world. Chinese children go to kindergarten when they are three years old. They start primary school when they are seven.

Most Chinese women go out to work. Very young children go to nurseries while their mothers are working. Sometimes they are looked after by their grandparents. The family is very important in China.

Many Chinese people get up early in the morning to do exercises before work. These exercises are called taiji, or "Chinese shadow boxing." People do them in the streets and parks.

This picture shows some Chinese
stamps and money. The units of
money are yuan, jiao and fen. There
are 100 fen in a yuan and 10 fen in a
jiao.

6

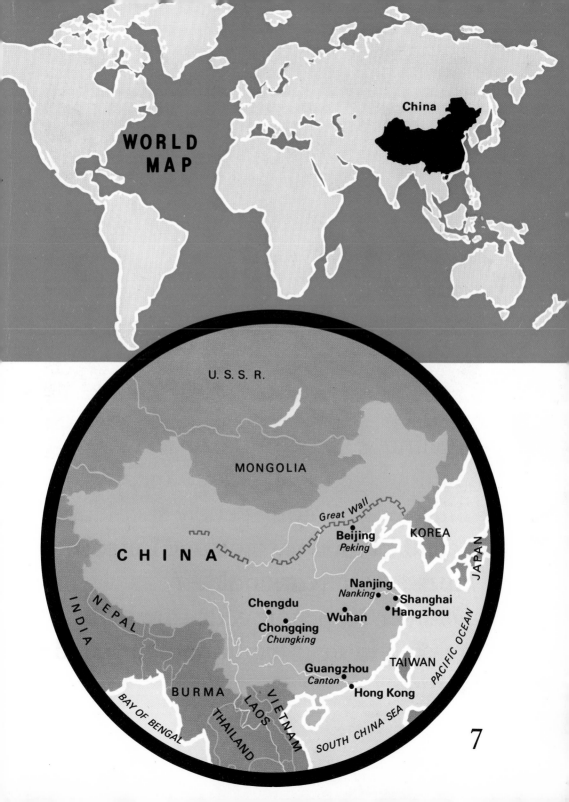

WORLD MAP

China

U.S.S.R.

MONGOLIA

Great Wall

Beijing
Peking

KOREA

JAPAN

CHINA

INDIA

NEPAL

Nanjing
Nanking

Chengdu

Shanghai
Hangzhou

Wuhan

Chongqing
Chungking

TAIWAN

PACIFIC OCEAN

Guangzhou
Canton

BURMA

Hong Kong

BAY OF BENGAL

LAOS

VIETNAM

THAILAND

SOUTH CHINA SEA

7

China is the world's largest country. Nearly everyone speaks Chinese. But many people speak a second language, such as Mongol or Tibetan. On National Day (October 1), people celebrate by dressing in their traditional national costumes.

The government, which is communist, owns all the land in China. Many Chinese boys and girls belong to a communist youth group. It is called The Young Pioneers. Members of the group wear red scarves around their necks.

There are no privately-owned cars in China. Most people have bicycles. The streets are crowded with cyclists and buses. Policemen direct traffic from platforms in the middle of the streets.

In the towns and cities of China there are huge department stores. They sell thousands of things made in China. This store in Beijing (Peking) sells enamel bowls.

Tea is grown in southern China. Chinese people drink a great deal of tea, without milk. Rice is also grown in flooded fields called paddy fields. Rice is a very important food in China.

Chinese people go shopping every day for food to make sure it is fresh. They go to street markets which sell vegetables and meat brought from the countryside. They often buy live fish and crabs.

13

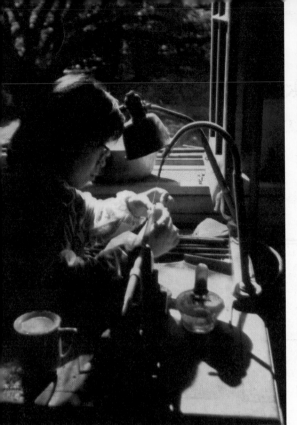

China has many traditional arts and crafts. Skilled workers produce silk embroidery, wood and stone carvings and other beautiful things. There are special craft workshops which make these goods in the city of Shanghai.

14

Chinese people like going to see acrobats, dancing and operas. The Red Silk Dance is a popular traditional folk dance in China.

Buddhism is one of the religions of
China. Few young Chinese people
now are religious, but there are
still many beautiful Buddhist
temples to visit. Shown here is a
statue of Buddha.

The Liu Ho Pagoda is in
Hangzhou. It has 13 floors and is
built of wood and brick. Pagodas
are temples. They were built in
China hundreds of years ago. They
marked holy places.

Most people in the larger towns live in flats which often have two or three rooms. Sometimes three generations of a family (grandparents, parents and children) live together in one flat.

Beijing is the capital of China. Tiananmen Square in Beijing can hold nearly a million people. Pictures of Chinese leaders decorate one side of the square.

China was once a great empire. Many emperors lived in Beijing's Imperial Palace. It was called the Forbidden City because ordinary people were not allowed inside. The Palace was built over 500 years ago and today has many museums.

20

Fierce-looking bronze lions stand in the Imperial Palace and in other old buildings in China. The lion was the symbol of the Emperors of China.

More than two-thirds of the Chinese people live in the countryside and work on the land. The houses in the villages are built of earth or stone bricks and have earth floors. Pigs and chickens wander in the village streets.

In China all the workers in the towns and countryside live and work in groups called communes. The communes, which are based in towns and larger villages, organize housing and schools for their members. Some run small factories.

In Beijing there are narrow side streets called hutungs. People live in houses built around courtyards. The houses have only one floor.

The People's Daily is the most important newspaper in China. In the towns copies of the newspaper are put up so that anyone may read the news.

Shanghai is the largest city in China. It is also an important port. Ships from all over the world come there. Junks are traditional Chinese boats with large sails. They are still used along the coast and down the rivers. Junks often dock alongside great tankers and modern cargo ships.

Many streets in China have slogans above them written in large characters. There are thousands of Chinese characters. The drawing represents the word China or "middle of the world." 中

Chinese food is served in small pieces and is eaten with chopsticks and spoons. Beijing Duck is a famous Chinese dish. It is eaten on special occasions.

At lunchtime many Chinese people eat rice and vegetables or steamed bread. The bread is sold from shops and stalls in the street.

Chinese people work hard and have few holidays. In their free time they play sports or relax in beautiful parks.

Chinese civilization goes back over 3,500 years. The Great Wall of China is 2,000 miles (3,200 km) long. It was built 2,000 years ago to protect northern China from her enemies.

Index